Printed in the United States of America

First Printing, 2013

ISBN - 13: 978-1492393054
ISBN - 10:1492393053

Acknowledgments:

I would like to express my gratitude to the many people who inspired me to keep writing:

My family, My friends at Immaculate, Betty, Mr. Nesbitt, Sarah J., Shihan Jim, Oma and Opa, Grandma June, Uncle Billy and Aunt Rachel

I dedicate this book to my mom and dad.

Contents

Gravity

When apples fell upon his head,

It's knowledge Isaac Newton got.

Today a boulder knocked me flat-

I must've really learned a lot.

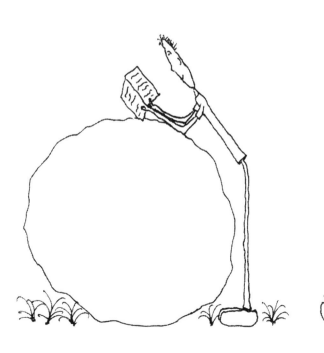

I Must Smell Pretty Good

A bee is standing on my toe.
I'm sitting with a buffalo.
The snapping turtle's lying on my head.
A tiger's snoozing in my lap:
So then if I as much as tap,
The tiger wakes, eats lunch then goes to bed.

There's something stalking from behind.
I sneak a peek but just to find
A pack of lions playing some prey game.
A hippo's dancing on my knee.
This must end in catastrophe.
The hippo keeps on dancing all the same.

I wish they'd all just take a hike.
I wonder when they're gonna strike.
I wonder if that bee will sting my feet.
I wish for something I could say
To make them simply go away.
But I'll just have to wait for them to eat.

The Deadly Sniffles

My elephant's sick from the peanuts he ate-

He sniffled and snortled all day.

But nothing compared with the mishap tonight:

He inhaled... and sneezed us away.

Music

Music soothes the savage beast,

so when I tried to play

the trumpet for a grizzly bear

it wasn't a good day.

Counterclockwise

My clock goes counterclockwise.
It hangs up on the wall.
It goes around and spins all day,
But makes no sense at all.
It goes from 10 to 9.
It runs from 4 to 3.
It ticks from 6 to 5.
It just confuses me.

I really wish that clock
Would stop and turn around.
It mocks me everyday
With that dumb old ticking sound.
I wish that it would leave.
I want it off that wall!
My clock goes counterclockwise.
It makes no sense at all.

Socks

They're neither lefties nor a right.

They hug your feet all snug and tight.

A tool that beats a socket wrench.

Except you won't prefer the stench.

The Hippo's Sweet Tooth

The hippopotami are crashing,
Running, raging through the town.
The hippopotami are bashing,
Making buildings topple down.

The hippopotami are coming,
Breaking down my bedroom door.
The hippopotami have learned that
I live in the candy store.

Insect School

The insects went to insect school
to learn about themselves.
They crawled right in and found a seat
and got books off the shelves.
The dragonflies were flapping their
large, fascinating wings.
The moths were waving round their big,
long, weird antenna - things.
They started learning 'bout the flies,
the bugs, the ticks, and fleas.
They started learning 'bout spiders,
some butterflies and bees.
They started learning 'bout bed bugs
and different types of ants.
They started learning 'bout what bugs
eat, what assorted plants.
And then they went to lunch and they
all brought a separate dish.
Then someone yelled "A human's coming!"
"Quick, run awa..."   Squish.

Collapse

I once built a house out of wood.

I finished and saw that it stood.

But it fell with a crash,

and a bang, and a bash,

so I guess it was not very good.

ABC

ABCD what comes next?
Q or H or M or X?
It's hard to figure out this set
when I don't know the alphabet.

The Other World

A whole 'nother world is behind that red door.
I walked in and saw it myself.
With slimy and gooey stuff slopped on the floor.
And nothing but junk on the shelf.

There isn't a sun so the sky is all black.
You must use a flashlight to see.
Most everyone carries a weight on their back.
The alphabet goes up to P.

The animals aren't like most creatures you know.
And most of them haven't been named.
They've never been put - with success - in a show
'Cause they haven't ever been tamed.

That world is all stinky and coated with grime.
There isn't one doctor or nurse.
You must plug your nose almost all of the time.
But sadly my room is much worse.

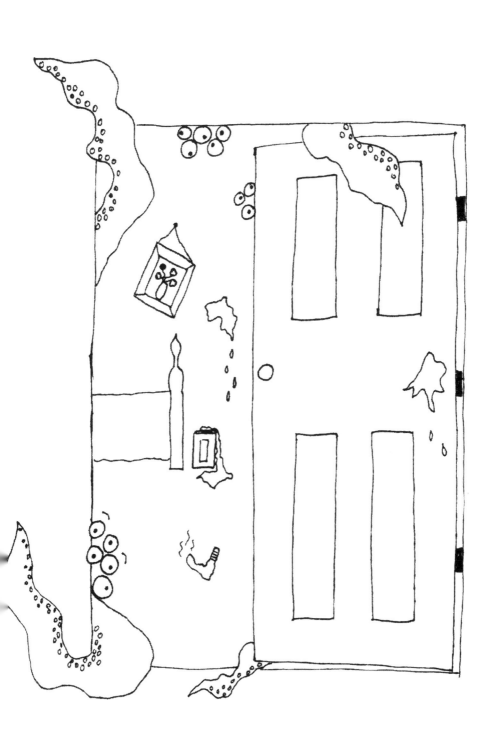

The Vampire Bat

The vampire bat

Ate the dog and the cat.

They wanted a way to avenge.

So the dog and the cat

Turned to zombies and that

Is how they ate bats in revenge.

My Pet Clouds

I have a pet cloud in my basement.
I feed it three times everyday.
I ran out of food for it last night.
It started to thunder today.

I've noticed it's gotten much bigger,
Then shrunk to it's regular size.
Then I saw little clouds with it-
Each with cute, baby- blue eyes!

I love all my clouds in the basement.
They're wonderful pets, with no fleas.
Today I went out and released them,
And watched as they blew in the breeze.

Our Tree's Party

We gathered around for the party.

Our tree was 100 years old.

We knew that it felt quite accomplished.

We knew that it felt very bold.

We quickly gave out all our presents.

We hardly could wait for dessert.

The tree was so happy to see it:

A plate full of water and dirt.

Abyss

I'm falling down a hole.

It's been this way for days.

I wonder when I'll ever benefit.

As boring as it is,

I don't think that I want,

To find the other end of

this deep pit.

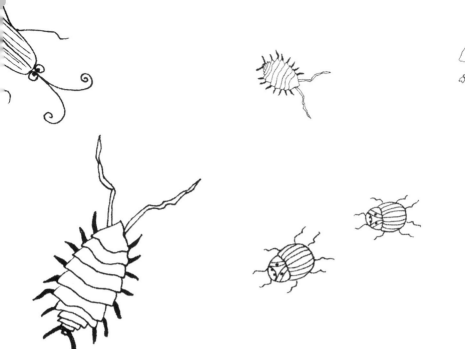

My Passion For Pets

Kittens are wonderful creatures.

Puppies, I love to give hugs.

Parrots are perfectly awesome.

I don't have a passion for bugs.

Careful Carl

Carl was carefully crossing the street
when he stopped to look both ways.
The cars kept coming so then he
stood there for 156 days.

He stood and he stood
and as the days flew,
he slowly then turned 102.

And just when he thought on his rules he'll depend,
the world slowly came to a horrible end.

Asteroids were falling,
stars came around,
people were running,
the trees melted down.

Carl was made of nothing but dust.
The world was now dead except for some rust.
Carl just sat, feeling totally beat.
So then he decided to cross the street.

If I Were

If I were a mockingbird I'd stop and sing.

If I were a ladybug I'd flap my wing.

If I were a bumblebee I'd sniff a rose.

If I were a woodpecker I'd break my nose.

The Man–Eating Lemon

I once was attacked by the man – eating lemon.
A ravenous, blood – thirsty brute.
It snuck up from behind, I had no time to find
Any shelter from this rotten fruit.

It opened its mouth showing jaws full of teeth!
They were sharp and acidulous too.
It backed me up into a wall where I feared
All the things that this lemon could do!

I closed my eyes, thinking the lemon would bite,
Then something outrageous occurred.
The terrible turnip jumped out of the trees
With some claws like the ones on a bird!

The terrible turnip! I thought to myself.
The man – eating lemon's one foe.
watched as they quarreled and argued and fought
And I saw that the violence would grow.

Eventually, after much punching and pain,
The terrible turnip had won.
But during its fighting, the turnip grew tired
And left, for its business was done.

My Tiger's Misbehaving

My tiger's misbehaving
For it's eaten all my fish.
My chicken and my turkey
Have been gobbled from my dish.

The bacon has been taken
And it ate my luscious steak.
The beef and pork are off my fork
I don't know what to make.

My tiger's eaten so much food
I don't know what he'll steal.
I think it's time that I consider
Veggies for a meal.

But then one afternoon when I
Was eating broccoli:
My tiger really had a feast,
It ate a scrumptious ME.

I Found a Fluffy Floofer

I found a fluffy floofer and I couldn't help but grin.
Its purple fur and noses are so cute.
I think that I will keep it and I'll call it Floofaflin.
I'll teach it speech and how to play the flute.

His fluffy fur is super fun to brush and comb and style.
It's pretty great to give him apples too.
I think that I will sit here and I'll feed him for a while.
I'm never bored, there's always stuff to do.

Of all the things I could've found, this floofer is the best.
I've never been this happy in the past.
But my floofer has a quality that sticks out from the rest.
My floofer reproduces much too fast.

When

When mules use tools, when horses fly

When clocks wear socks, when pigs make pie

When shoes sing blues, when clouds fall down

When chairs grow hair, when peppers frown

When plants use pants, when lights read books

When trees eat bees, when dogs cast hooks

When figs wear wigs, when frogs wear vests

That's when I'll ace my grammar test.

My Lizard's Growing Up

My hairy lizard has a beard.
He has a mustache too.
My mother thinks he's kind of weird.
I don't know what to do.

Whenever people see my pet
They're sure to stop and stare.
I don't think it's a problem yet.
He just has lots of hair.

My mother stopped me at the door
(Her eyes did seem to gleem.)
She said that she went to the store
And bought some shaving cream.

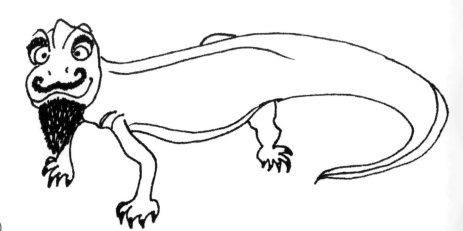

Spelling

When it comes to spelling bees

all I can spell is "a"

and "I" and "an" and "the" and "and"

and "cat" and "hat" and "hay"

and "hi" and "bye" and "mat"

and "wall" and "pan" and "pot" and "birds."

Actually I'd win a bee for tiny little words.

Spider Man

I saw the movie Spider Man

but I don't get the plot.

Today a spider bit me

and a rash was all I got.

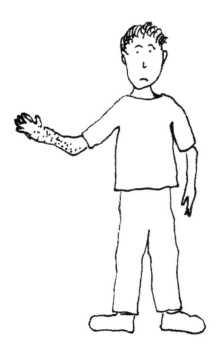

That's What I Thought

I thought that I could play a song,

I tried it all, even the gong.

But from my friends I heard no cheers,

Instead they covered up their ears.

Strange Day

Today was a very strange day.

It started out just like it should.

I fed my blue whale

And then combed up my tail,

Then I ate my whole wheat bowl of wood.

I plugged in my radio set,

And tuned it to watch a nice show.

I lay on the chair

And I slept on the stair

Then I terribly stubbed my ring toe.

But right around 18 o'clock,

I snacked when my dinner was near.

I ran out of trout

So I made it without.

Now wouldn't you call that quite queer?

Outlet

The outlet made a frowning face
and gazed on up at me.
It did not look very happy
as far as I could see.
I did not like that frowning face
I wanted it to go.
So I just did a simple thing:
plugged in the radio.

Special Thanks

I give a thanks to all the things
That help me through my day.
For instance I just thanked the plants
that help me breath ok.

And when I need to wash my plates
I thank my soapy sponger.
But now I give a special thanks
right to my trusty plunger.

Freedom

I looked in confusion up high.

A penguin was soaring up there.

I heard myself saying "Oh my!"

"A penguin up high in the air!"

Meanwhile the penguin, of course,

Was thrilled with his new point of view.

He spotted a little brown horse

Then up through a white cloud he flew.

No longer will this bird be flightless.

Like ostrich, emu and kiwi.

No longer will this bird be mightless.

This penguin could fly, he was free!

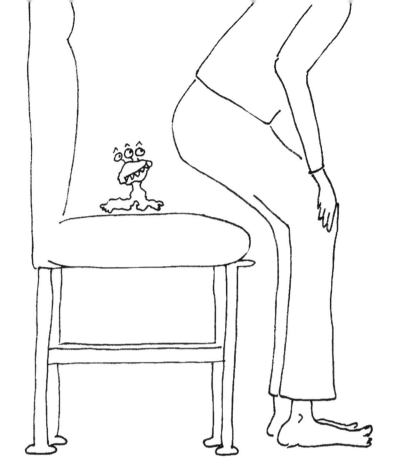

Strange Creature

I tried to sit down in a chair
but something else was sitting there.
It was tiny and bright blue.
It had large feet and sharp fangs too.
It had three eyes all seaweed green.
It wanted food and had no spleen.
Although this was a splendid find,
It nearly chomped on my behind.

Salt

Why is salt in all the seas?

Now I know just why!

God had some along with lunch

and dropped it from the sky.

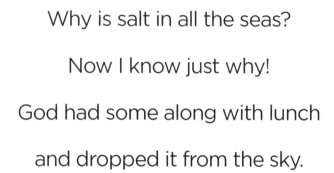

My Home

The TV's broke, the couch is old.

My bright red apples now have mold.

The fridge is warm, the freezer hot.

There is a spider in my cot.

The floor's a mess, the books are torn.

In my house beetles have been born.

The chair is crushed, the window smashed.

My new computer has just crashed.

Upon the table is a hen.

I think it's time to move again.

Shadow

My shadow walked right up to
me and kindly said hello.
It asked for somewhere warm to stay,
because of all the snow.
:ook it to my house where I then stifled a big yawn.
I went to bed, turned off the lights,
and now my shadow's gone.

The Places I've Been

I've come from a lot of weird places,
With grasses of purple and pink.
With lizard and anteater races,
And creatures who terribly stink.

They sleep on the floor or the ceiling,
And swim through the air over trees.
They eat things you don't find appealing,
And bathe in the honey of bees.

And all of those smelly weird creatures,
They love to be told stories too.
Despite their disgusting green features,
I kindly tell them about you.

I've seen all their gasping and crying,
They think it's completely absurd.
They think I am fibbing and lying,
But love the good stories they've heard.

Roses

I picked a rose up off the ground.

It started bleeding, drooping down.

The stem was ripping and it tore.

I don't pick roses anymore.

Scentimental

Said the tree to the smelly skunk,
"You're looking ill, hop in my trunk."

o the tree took the skunk to the doctor who said,
"Sit down, you're sick. Rest in this bed."

He was sick for quite some time.
The kind tree paid for every dime.

Eventually the doctor said,
"I'm sorry tree, but he is dead."

A shame that he will not revive,
The skunk stunk worse dead than alive.

Electric

I have an electrical puppy.

I have an electrical plant.

I have an electrical kitten.

I have an electrical aunt.

I have an electrical blanket.

I have an electrical door.

I have an electrical pillow.

I have an electrical floor.

I have an electrical picture.

I have an electrical gate.

I have an electrical playground.

I love the year 6008!

Piano Keys

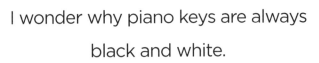

I wonder why piano keys are always

black and white.

I asked them all, but no one ever said.

If I were he who made that loud,

perplexing instrument,

I think I'd take a go at blue and red.

Ants

I saw a little ant today.
I screamed and ran in fright.
For I've heard that they're vicious things
and sometimes even bite.

My parents asked me why I screamed
at tiny little ants.
I told them you would also scream
if they once roamed your pants.

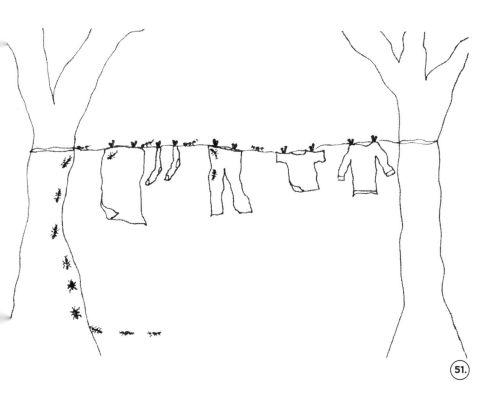

While Seaching
For a Penny

While searching for a penny in a snowstorm on the moon,

I found a creature I did not expect:

An herbivore, gregarious, insomniac baboon!

This, I thought, I surely must inspect!

But right before I did this thing, a wild shnimmer came.

It brought a shlup, the flirshiest I've seen.

"I think that these fine creatures need observing."
I proclaimed.

I got a magnifying glass of green.

And then they all attacked me with some sticks that they h
brought.

I suspected they would eat me very soon.

As they put me over fire and then chanted things I though

What a lousy trip up to the moon.

Galactic Controversy

Today I saw a sight to see:

A Galactic Controversy.

It broke the moon and shook the stars.

It caused a crater right on Mars.

I guess that happens for I ate

Space Blasters last night, really late.

My Secret Chimpanzee

I've got a secret chimpanzee.
I keep him in my room.
He makes a mess, I clean it up
With soap and rags and brooms.

And I'll say my chimpanzee
Is actually none other
Than my stinky, sticky, smelly, icky
Dirty little brother.

Life

I squiggle, I wiggle, I like dirt, I squirm.

A bird comes, I'm eaten, that's life for a worm.

I Am Flying Through the Sky

I am flying through the sky.

I don't know exactly why.

Something just came over me,

Then I flew right past the sea.

Crows and seagulls stopped and cooed

At my super altitude.

The things I saw! The views I had!

I could even see my dad!

I could see my house from there,

As I soared right through the air.

People stared and wondered why,

I was flying through the sky.

Alone

My parents are leaving me alone at home.
That means I can use my mom's favorite comb.
I'll jump on my bed and run through the house.
I'll ride on the cat while he's chasing a mouse.
I'll watch my favorite TV show all night.
I'll have a party and we'll dance till it's light.
I'll run right outside where I'll climb all the trees.
I'll break a beehive and out will come bees.
I'll eat all the junk food that I can consume.
I'll light the fireworks and they will go boom.
When my parents get home from where they wer
I'll have to listen to my punishment.

Babies

The baby's crying, he won't stop.

But why? I couldn't tell.

And then he smiled, I was happy.

I ignored the smell.

The Tooth

Sometimes there are teeth that just never come out
That happened to someone named Caroline Clout.
She'd pry and she'd pull and she'd want to shout,
Just 'cause of that tooth that would never come out

She tried for long years to get that tooth out.
Everyone helped her, even some trout.
Sometimes she would seriously doubt,
That she would ever get that tooth out.

Then one day she sat down to pout,
She bit an apple and it came out!
And that night in her mouth did sprout,
A brand new tooth for her to pull out.

The Scarecrow

"I'm finally scary!" the scarecrow proclaimed,

"The boy came here, then ran away!"

But sadly it wasn't the scarecrow's mean looks.

The boy was allergic to hay.

The Chalkboard is Filled

The chalkboard is filled with the things
That I need to memorize soon.
I need to know how a bird sings.
And when we last went to the moon.
I need to remember the date
Of Theodore Roosevelt's birth.
I need to remember how much
8,000,000 quarters are worth.

I need to know how many pies
The worlds greatest baker can make.
I must know the meaning of nigh,
Gadzookery, gimbals and schnake.
I've got to remember the flags
Of China, Japan and Peru.
I haven't remembered a thing.
I guess I have homework to do.

My Garden is Peculiar

My bean plant gives me jellybeans
I serve them on a tray.
From blues to blacks and greys to greens
I harvest them all day.

And people pay to see my plant
It's truly very rare.
My neighbors (who are gardeners)
Don't really think it's fair.

There's something else about me that
Is surely not my fault.
My pepper plant gives pepper
But it also gives me salt.

Fran's Fan

Fran fans Fran's hands
With Fran's fan.
Fran's got one fan
And two hands.

Fran fans one hand
At a time.
When Fran fans, Fran
Feels sublime.

What Happened?

"What happened?" my mom asked me
as I came all teary eyed.
"Did you scrape your knee on something,
has your new pet goldfish died?
Did you fail your final spelling test
or fall out of your bed?
Did your very special notebook tear
or did you hit your head?
Did you get a cramp upon your foot
or stub your pinky toe?"
"Nope", I answered to my mom
"I missed my favorite show."

Is That a Zombie?

Is that a zombie on the bed?
Is that a disconnected head?
Is that a hairy handprint on the door?
And I have not the slightest clue
To what I am supposed to do
About the clammy creature on the floor.

Is that a monster sleeping there?
There's something creeping in my hair!
Count Dracula's not helping with my fear.
A werewolf's howling at the moon.
I hope they all leave sometime soon.
I wish those witches wouldn't sit so near.

I'm terrified inside my toes.
I'm horrified inside my nose.
I'm scared in every place that's in between.
I wish I had a happy pill.
I'm frightened silly up until
My sister chuckles "Happy Halloween!"

This Plate of Goo

My mother handed me some greens.
I sighed and looked at her.
"I'd eat a lot of healthy things,
but this I don't prefer."

"You cannot make me eat this plate
of icky rancid goo.
Not now, at least, I'll think of when.
This much I promise you."

"How 'bout I eat this dinner
in one hundred fifty years?
So see, I'll still be eating it.
There's no need for your tears."

"I cannot wait to eat this stuff!
I'll have it with some tea.
This icky yucky plate of goo
you kindly made for me."

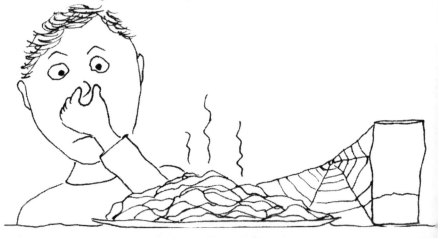

Frankenstein's Employment

When Frankenstein came back to life
He had to find a job.
He found employment at a store
That sold some shish ka bob.

He ate the food and lost that job.
His boss called him a joke.
He couldn't find another one
So Frankenstein went broke.

Christmas for the Teacher

Today is the school day
before Christmas break.
Our teacher prepared an
assignment to take.
She said that we all had
to go to the store,
and buy a big seashell
that came from the shore.
And buy a new ipod,
a tea cup, a cat,
a TV with HD,
a pink skirt, a hat,
a DS, a Wii game,
a CD, a phone,
a jacket, a good book,
a mint ice cream cone,
some lipstick, a nice dress,
a dog with soft fur,
then wrap them in gift wrap
and give them to her.

Shells

Our family went to the beach

And I looked for some shells.

I looked and looked and looked so long

That I let out a yell.

I couldn't find one anywhere.

I know I would've shrieked.

But finally I found a shell

(just not the kind I seeked.)

I Forgot Something
This Morning...

I breathed on a flower, it died.
I breathed on my brother, he cried.
I breathed on my sister
She got a big blister.
I breathed on my mother, she sighed.

I breathed on my teacher, she fled.
I breathed on a cobra, it shed.
I breathed on my chili
It ran willie nilllie.
I breathed on a beetle, it's dead.

I breathed on the blue sky, it rained.
I breathed on a T-shirt, it stained.
I breathed on a pencil
It made out a stencil
That said, "BRUSH YOUR TEETH,

YOU BONEBRAIN!"

The Monster of Blicker

The monster of Blicker", my grandpa once said,
"is seldom a kind-hearted beast."
"For if you should fight it you'd surely be dead,
It'd find you a wonderful feast."

"It isn't a dragon, though it does breathe fire.
It's something a thousand times worse.
If he chose to torch you in murk and the mire,
You'd need something more than a nurse."

"I do not believe in this big Blicker beast!"
I said, feeling that I was sure.
I wasn't bamboozled of fooled in the least.
But what was that deafening roar?

Sir Trishin the Magician

Sir Trishin the Magician
Performed magic far and near.
He'd read your mind and always find
A coin behind your ear.

Sir Trishin the Magician
Could pull rabbits out of hats.
He produced a box of kittens
Where there once had been black rats.

Sir Trishin the Magician
Could escape from cuffs and chains.
He levitates fifteen pound weights.
He always entertains.

Sir Trishin does a lot of tricks
To which the crowds are drawn.
But at the end of every show
He bows, then POOF, he's gone.

I Tried to Outwit My Computer

I tried to outwit my computer
At math, social studies and chess,
At history, science and spelling.
I found it was to my distress.

My fingers scrolled over the keyboard,
Attempting to beat this machine.
I clicked everything I could think of,
But failure was shown on the screen.

Frustration began to take over.
My mental controls went *kersplat*.
But then, I **DID** beat that contraption.
Just not with my mind but a bat.

The Glomatt

Sir Jiliby Fett
Has the silliest pet,
A strange little thing called a Glomatt.
Part camel, part bird,
It's really absurd,
And comes from a far away comet.

To own one of these
You must sail overseas
To the island named Bangalaflet.
Once there you will find
Many more of its kind,
And you'll have an amazing new pet.

Giving

Today was Christmas morning
And I got a lot of toys.
A helicopter, robot and
Some things that just make noise.

In fact, I have so many toys
They won't fit in my room.
I feel afraid that one more toy
Will cause an awful boom.

I'm tired of this getting thing.
It's getting kind of old.
I'm gonna try some giving.
It feels jolly, I've been told.

So I stopped the boring getting
And I tried a bit of giving.
I feel happy now, so happy!
Oh, today I started living!

Floofer FUN

1. What color is a Floofer?

2. What time is it when you run out of trout?

3. Who races with lizards?

4. What year will you get an electrical puppy?

5. What is the flirshiest?

6. What breathes fire?

7. Who lost her tooth?

8. What happens when figs wear wigs?

9. Who is the man-eating lemon's one foe?

10. How old was Careful Carl?

11. Where is the snapping turtle sitting?

12. What was on the table when it was time to move?

13. Who has the silliest pet?

Answers:

1. Purple   2. 18 O'clock   3. Anteaters   4. 6008   5. A Shlup   6. The Monster of Blicker
7. Caroline Clout   8. I'll ace my test   9. The terrible turnip   10. 102
11. On my head   12. A hen   13. Sir Jilliby Fett

Santino can often be found practicing piano, eating pizza, and perfecting his punctuation in the sixth grade.

He resides in Western New York with his parents, little brother, and big sister.

If you would like to write to Santino, or are interested in finding out more about his work, you can reach him at :
monkeytino@gmail.com

Made in the USA
Charleston, SC
16 November 2013